first
putting GOD first in living and giving

Devotions

Program Components

Book
shiny gods: finding freedom from things that distract us

DVD
shiny gods: finding freedom from things that distract us
Video programs with downloadable leader guide

Program Flash Drive with Booklet
first: putting GOD first in living and giving
Instructions for planning and using the program

Devotions
first: putting GOD first in living and giving
Daily meditations to use during the program

Youth Study Edition
first: putting GOD first in living and giving
Book for youth to use during the program, with leader helps

Children's Leader Guide
first: putting GOD first in living and giving
Lesson plans for younger and older children

Program Kit
first: putting GOD first in living and giving
One of each component

Mike Slaughter

first

putting GOD first in living and giving

Devotions
by Matthew L. Kelley

Abingdon Press
Nashville

Mike Slaughter

first:
putting GOD first in living and giving

Devotions
by Matthew L. Kelley

This book is printed on acid-free paper.

ISBN 978-1-4267-6202-4

Scripture quotations, unless otherwise indicated, are from the Common English Bible, © Copyright 2010 by Common English Bible, and are used by permission.

Scripture quotations marked NRSV are taken from the New Revised Standard Version of the Bible, copyright 1989, Division of Christian Education of the National Council of the Churches of Christ in the United States of America. Used by permission. All rights reserved.

Scriptures marked KJV are from the King James or Authorized Version of the Bible.

Library of Congress Cataloging-in-Publication applied for.

13 14 15 16 17 18 19 20 21 22—10 9 8 7 6 5 4 3 2 1

MANUFACTURED IN THE UNITED STATES OF AMERICA

Contents

Week Three
Be Faithful, Save, and Give

Week Four
Heart Giving

Introduction

Welcome! Thank you for participating in the stewardship program *first: putting GOD first in living and giving*. I pray that these daily devotions, along with your reading of Mike Slaughter's book, *shiny gods: finding freedom from things that distract us*, will enhance your experience of being challenged in your stewardship over the next month.

Let's be honest: Money is an uncomfortable subject. How we spend our money is an important and telling expression of priorities in our lives, and most of us don't like to acknowledge the gap between the values we think we should have and those we actually have.

The goal of this stewardship program in your church is not to make you feel guilty, nor is it to say that you have to be exactly like this or that person. The goal is for all of us to ask hard questions of ourselves and be open to the possibility that God will lead us in new directions in our lives.

Over the next four weeks, we'll be challenged in a number of different ways. We'll be asked to look for the idols in our own lives (most of them aren't animals made of gold) and name the ways that they enslave us, holding us back from living in the true freedom that God desires for us.

We'll be challenged to consider the place that money, work, and debts have in our own lives. What are our common understandings of these, and might the witness of Scripture lead us to some different understandings?

We'll be challenged to ask ourselves what it means for us to be faithful, to save, and to give. How do we balance all the competing interests in our lives? What priorities does God want us to have?

Finally, we'll be challenged to give with our hearts, not out of obligation or a sense of duty and not just when we think the recipient deserves our gift. Instead, we'll be challenged to give the way God gives—freely, fully, with no favorites or expectations of repayment.

It is my prayer that, at the end of these four weeks, we will have begun to grow into the individuals and the church that God knows we can be. May these devotions help you to put God first in your own living and giving.

Matthew L. Kelley

Week One

NAMING OUR IDOLS

1. AFTER THE PROMISE

Exodus 20:2-4, 22-24; 32:1-35

God doesn't like idols. God made that abundantly clear when the Israelites were at Mt. Sinai and God gave them his top-ten list describing the kind of nation he was calling them to be. No idols. Okay, got it. No sweat, right? Except that a few chapters later, there was this giant gold statue of a cow in the center of a big, wild party, while God and Moses were up on the mountain working out the fine print of the covenant. How did the Israelites go from a grateful nation of liberated slaves gladly receiving God's law one minute, to a restless group dancing around an idol the next?

Well, old habits die hard. The Hebrews had lived all their lives in Egypt, where they had seen people make sacrifices to their gods. Given how wealthy the Egyptians were, the sacrifices must have seemed to the Hebrews like a good strategy, so when they faced their own time of uncertainty in the wilderness it makes sense that they fell back on what they knew. Except that this strategy was exactly the opposite of what God wanted, and God was not happy about it.

Even more basic than old habits dying hard, though, was the fact that it's easier to put your faith in something you can see. You can wrap your mind around it. And because you can understand it, you feel some measure of control over it. By contrast, it's a whole lot harder to put your faith in an abstract idea and to keep it there when things get rough. That was exactly the challenge that these newly liberated slaves faced.

Yes, the Israelites saw God unleash plagues on Egypt and part the seas for them to escape the Egyptian cavalry. But then Moses went up on the mountain, and the people were just supposed to wait, and there were very few clues about how to find sustainable sources of food and water. They were simply supposed to trust this invisible God, who was going to get around to finishing the job whenever he got around to it. At least, that's how it must have seemed.

Given the circumstances, it makes sense that they thought the easiest way forward was to take the gold they had plundered on their way out of Egypt (that the invisible God had provided for them, ironically enough), ask Aaron to melt it down, and make an idol to see what would happen. It must have seemed more proactive than waiting around and doing nothing.

Aaron knew better, of course, but when everyone kept pressuring him, he gave in. He built the idol, even though he knew it was a bad idea. Maybe he thought it could be done before Moses returned, and Moses and God would be none the wiser. Oops.

What seems like a strange, foreign story to us in the modern world becomes a lot more understandable when we break it down to its most basic, human elements. Maybe we've seen God do great things, maybe even experienced them personally. We've been enthralled by the stories of those who have given up everything, trusted God completely, and been part of something incredible. And those stories might have lit a fire in us, causing us to make a commitment to live differently, to trust God and give as generously as we can.

But then reality sets in. We see people losing their homes and their life savings when the housing bubble bursts and the stock market crashes. We feel the pinch when the cost of gas goes up, and we see that the people around us who seem to be doing well are the ones who played it safe, who didn't take big risks and are sitting on a nice rainy-day fund. Maybe no one is actively urging us to join the crowd the way they did to Aaron, but we hear the message loud and clear. We're tempted to go back on our commitment to trust God and to return to faith in things we can see, touch, and control.

Naming our idols involves acknowledging the power they hold, power we feel even after we've named them as idols and promised to turn away from them. As you prayerfully consider the idols in your own life, remember what the Israelites learned: that the idols will still tempt you even after you turn from them. But also remember that the God who delivers you from their power will give you the strength to resist them. Place your faith in the one who remains after the idols have turned to dust.

Lord, help me to recognize the idols that hold power in my own life. Give me the courage to name them and the strength to turn away, even as others around me continue to worship them. Amen.

2. Taking the Long View

Deuteronomy 4:12-15; 2 Kings 17:24-41; Matthew 6:19-24

We humans are a pretty shortsighted lot. We tend to focus only on the here and now, what we can see, touch, and understand. Sure, we know that there is a future beyond this moment, but that's not as real to us as what's right in front of us. We have a hard time taking the long view.

Maybe it's not entirely our fault. After all, we are inherently limited, finite beings. What we perceive with our five senses is what is most real to us. We grasp time in relatively short spans. I can understand that what I do now will affect my life five years from now. I can understand the need to save for retirement. I can even kinda sorta understand that one day I will die. But it's hard.

We humans might be short-term thinkers, but God challenges us not to settle just for what we can wrap our minds around. Worshiping what we can create and control is what got Israel in trouble in the wilderness, and sadly, it wasn't the last time. When Moses gave his farewell address to the people before they crossed the Jordan, he reminded them that they never "saw" God during their forty years of wandering. God spoke to them through a fire, something powerful and extremely hard to control. He challenged them not to settle just for what they knew, but to trust the God who was beyond full comprehension, and certainly beyond their ability to control. In other words, Moses told the people to let God be in charge.

But did they listen? Of course not! Israel's history, like our history, is a roller coaster. People focus on what they can control, find out it doesn't work, cry to God for help, see God save the day, worship God faithfully for a while, then lose focus and lose faith, and the whole process starts all over again.

Centuries after Moses, the Israelites were living in the Promised Land, but the Northern and Southern Kingdoms had split, and the North had been overrun by the Assyrian empire. People from other lands had moved in and brought the worship of their gods with them. So the remaining Israelites chose to worship both their God and the foreign gods, basically as a way of hedging their bets. They figured that at least one of those would be the right god to pray to so the harvest would be good, and it in the process their worship of the other gods would help them get along with their neighbors. They were making their decisions based solely on what would help them right at that moment. In doing that, they were abandoning their faithfulness to the God who had delivered their ancestors from slavery.

Several centuries after that, Jesus was preaching to a large crowd and told them they needed to think long term. "Store up treasures in heaven," he said, and it remains true today. Sure, the latest gadget makes us happy right in the moment, but it's not long before it breaks down, isn't as shiny, gets stolen, or becomes obsolete once a new model comes out. Jesus urged us to sacrifice short-term comfort and build the kind of wealth that can't get stolen, won't fade away, and will never lose its luster.

What are the pressures of short-term thinking in your own life? Do you really want that shiny new car more than you want to invest in the kingdom of God through your church or some other organization? Does the stress of paying the bills or saving enough for retirement hold you back from a commitment to tithe? What would it mean for you to take the long view? What treasures in heaven could you be pursuing right now?

Lord, help me to know and resist the idols in my own life, and to invest in eternal treasures. Help me to see my actions in light of eternity, so that everything I do will be an act of worship to you. Amen.

3. UNLEARNING

Psalm 135:15-18

In the movie *The Matrix*, there is a great scene in which Neo, recently "unplugged" from a giant machine that uses human beings as batteries and awakened to the real world, is unlearning all the things he thought he knew. Morpheus, the leader of the rebel humans resisting the machines, is teaching Neo the new fighting skills that have been uploaded into his brain. After some amazing kung-fu sparring, Neo bends over, gasping for air, and says that Morpheus is too fast.

Morpheus replies, "Do you think that my being faster or stronger than you has anything to do with my muscles? You think that's air you're breathing?" Neo is still convinced that everything he is seeing at that moment is real, even though on some level he knows that he's inside a computer program. But knowing it in abstract and really believing it are two entirely different things. The rest of the film shows Neo's journey to let go of his illusions and grasp what is real.

The Matrix got people talking about deep philosophical and theological questions. How do we know what is real and what is not? Do we trust our senses, or can they be fooled as easily as in the movie? How do we know that what we *think* we know is in fact true?

Idols are like the machines in *The Matrix*. They're not as systematic, and maybe not as sinister, but their effect on us is just as harmful. The idols we worship and put in place of God turn us into something less than we were created to be. We end up giving our energy to something that sucks us dry and provides nothing in return. All that for something that's not even real!

The psalmist points out the folly of giving our worship to idols. Idols look real, but they can't hear our prayers or speak a word to answer them. They're shiny, but when you get down to it they're just atoms arranged in a certain way, no different from the dust that you swept out your door this morning. These idols aren't real. They're nothing. And when we worship nothing, we get nothing in return.

An idol—whether it's a statue, a job title, a desired salary level, or our dream house—can't give us real and lasting satisfaction, because it's not alive. It's not real. Only the living God can give us anything real and life-giving in return.

For us to get our priorities in line, we must unlearn many of the things we were taught about, like what is important in life. It's not enough to know in the abstract that money and power and status aren't the most important things in the world. We can say it all we want, but unless our actions match, they're just as empty and meaningless as the idols we're warned against worshiping.

In Neo's training to free his mind, Morpheus loads the "jump program," in which the two of them are on top of a tall building, and the task is to jump to the top of another tall building far away. Neo takes the leap, but he's so invested in gravity that his mind can't grasp the situation, and he slams into the pavement.

Have you ever found yourself in a situation where you suddenly realized your words and your actions didn't line up? How does it feel to be struck with the truth that you're not where you want to be in life? What are the idols that you know are idols but still have a grip on you? Has there ever been a point when you realized that whatever you were worshiping wasn't giving you anything in return?

Lord, I don't have the strength to let go of my idols on my own. Only you can help me do that. Help me to lay them aside and give my absolute best to you. Amen.

4. Uncomfortable Truths

Daniel 2:24-28, 3:7-30

All of us need people in our lives who are courageous enough to tell us uncomfortable truths. Many of us don't want to hear about things we need but don't want, and still fewer of us want to deal with the consequences of telling a truth that will upset a friend. People willing to resist those impulses and tell the truth are heroes.

Consider these four biblical heroes: Daniel, Shadrach, Meshach, and Abednego. These four young men were Jews who were carried off to Babylon after Jerusalem fell. They were identified as being among the best and brightest of the exiles, so they were selected to be trained in the language and culture of the empire, and to be given important positions in the imperial government. The logic of the empire was that it was not enough to have a military victory: The spirit of the conquered people must be broken by getting the most promising young people to turn their backs on the religion and culture of their birth and become Babylonians.

But these four young men showed incredible strength in resisting the empire's attempt to wipe out their culture. They stayed faithful to God, even though all their immediate circumstances (and more than a few people around them) said to give in. "Yeah, it stinks what happened to your home country, but that's your ancestors' fault, not yours. Just go through the motions of acknowledging these new gods while remaining loyal to the real God in your heart. It's a win-win situation."

But not Daniel, Shadrach, Meshach, and Abednego. They had the courage to remain loyal to the God of Israel and avoid doing anything that even remotely suggested otherwise. Their courage became even more impressive when they faced dire consequences for telling the truth.

King Nebuchadnezzar had been having some strange dreams that he wanted to have interpreted, and it just so happened that Daniel had the gift of interpreting dreams. Daniel had just seen the wisest men in Babylon executed for failing to interpret the dreams, so Daniel knew he should be careful about what he said. But when Daniel stood there before the king, he stated that the source of his gift is was the God of Israel, not the gods that Nebuchadnezzar worshiped. Pretty bold.

Shadrach, Meshach, and Abednego faced an even clearer choice. Everyone who didn't worship the golden statue would be thrown into a furnace. When the three of them were hauled before the king to explain their refusal to worship the statue, they replied that God might or might not rescue them, but they would not worship the idol. Thrown into the furnace, they were met by an angel and were not even singed. Their miraculous survival so impressed Nebuchadnezzar that he changed his mind and acknowledged the God of Israel.

Telling an uncomfortable truth in the face of strong opposition is not an easy or fun thing to do, but showing that kind of courage doesn't go unnoticed. Someone might get angry with you for taking a nonjudgmental, principled stand; but then again, they might just respect the courage it takes and consider the possibility that you're right.

What would it look like for you to resist the power of the idols around you and label them as such without condemning those who disagree with you?

If you and your coworkers are getting bonuses, and they're all planning to spend the money on a car or a boat, you might decide to contribute to your church's project to build an orphanage or dig wells in parts of the world where people die every day from a lack of clean drinking water.

If many of your friends are moving to bigger houses just because they can afford it, you might choose to remain where you are, being satisfied with having what you need and not accumulating more just because you are able to.

Maybe you have friends who are clearly orienting their priorities around making more money or getting promotions, and in doing so they are being dishonest or compromising a value they hold dear. In that moment, when you see the idol for what it is, can you muster the courage to challenge your friends' choices, lovingly, and invite them to withdraw their worship from that idol?

Whatever life situation you find yourself in, may you gain the courage to tell an uncomfortable truth, and the humility to listen when someone tells that truth to you.

Lord, help me to know and resist the idols in my own life. Give me the courage to resist their temptation, even when that resistance may cost me in the moment. Amen.

5. Taking Risks

Matthew 8:21-22

In Matthew 8, we see Jesus performing miracles, and because people are impressed, they want to follow him. Sounds like a great opportunity to grow the movement, right? This is Jesus' opportunity to expand his influence and change a lot of lives!

At least, that's our logic. It's certainly the logic of church growth! But Jesus, as usual, does what we least expect him to do. One guy comes and tells Jesus that he wants to join up, but that he needs to go and bury his father first. Jesus tells him quite bluntly to "let the dead bury their own dead."

Wait, what? Is Jesus telling a man to let his father's corpse rot? Can't Jesus let the guy catch up with the group in a day or two? Is Jesus really that insensitive?

Well, no. That's not quite what is going on here. Jesus is a preacher and sometimes tends to exaggerate, but this isn't one of those times. The issue here is about standard cultural expectations and practices.

This man's father probably isn't dead at the moment when his son has this conversation with Jesus. People in first-century Judean society were expected to keep their sick or aging family members in their homes and care for them until they died. There were no nursing homes or Social Security in Israel. You depended on your relatives to care for you when you couldn't take care of yourself anymore. So this man's father, though not dead, may have been living in his home and depending on his son to care for him during his senior years.

Understanding the culture of Jesus' time, which was very different from our own, helps us to understand what's going on here. Jesus is not being insensitive; rather, he is emphasizing the high cost of discipleship. No one in that family-oriented society would think less of the man for honoring his obligations toward his father, but Jesus knows that while this might be the man's excuse today, it will probably be something else tomorrow. There is always a practical concern that will convince us to play it safe. But if we feel God calling us, we must respond right then, even if it means taking a big risk.

"Gosh, I'd love to give a full ten percent of my income to the work of the Kingdom, but I've got this mortgage, and we're saving for the kids' college. Once I get that stuff under control, then I'll get serious about serving God."

"I feel called to give a year of my life to serve in an area with some serious needs, but I just graduated, and I'll have to start paying down these student loans. I'll get to that when my life is less crazy."

"Wow, that new ministry in our church sounds great, and I think it would be fulfilling to volunteer my time and energy to it—if I had any. You see, I need to pull some extra hours at work because I might get that big promotion, and I'm spending most of my spare time taking the kids from one activity to another. Yes, my whole family would benefit from being part of this ministry, but things are just too busy right now. We'll make time for it when we can."

There is always a good, practical reason to put off taking the risk of giving more to God. Few people will fault us for playing it safe. We've got to do what we've got to do. But we have to ask: When will all the complications in our lives be worked out? When will we be financially secure enough? When will we have enough time? The truth is that we won't, and we need to make some hard choices.

At some point, those immediate concerns cross the line from responsibilities to idols. Even though following Jesus may seem impractical or irresponsible, it is never a mistake. It's giving our worship to the one who deserves it, instead of to an ever-moving goal that we never will reach.

Lord, I have so many things that demand my loyalty, and they all seem really important. Help me to know what you are calling me to do, and to follow even if it seems impractical or irrational. Amen.

6. THE FIRST COMMANDMENT

Deuteronomy 4:12-15; 2 Kings 17:24-41; Matthew 6:19-24

One of the things that blew my mind in my Old Testament seminary class was that there was disagreement over how to number the Ten Commandments. Growing up, I saw that nearly every Sunday school room had a chart listing them. The first commandment was "I am the LORD thy God . . . . Thou shalt have none other gods before me. (KJV)" The second was "Thou shalt not take the name of the LORD thy God in vain," and our teachers explained to us that it meant using God's name as a curse word, the way some of us heard our dads doing later that afternoon if their favorite football team made a bad play.

What I learned in Old Testament class was that what I had always heard as two commandments might actually be three. Some sources say that the first commandment is simply "I am the LORD thy God." Wait a second, I thought; that doesn't make sense. "I am God" is a statement, not a commandment, right?

That's true only if we understand a commandment as either "Do this" or "Don't do that." There's a lot of that in the Mosaic Law, to be sure, but if we think of the Commandments not so much as a list of rules, but as a set of values that shape us at the very core of our being, then it makes sense for the first commandment to be a statement about God. God is God, and God likes it that way. Everything else in the Law flows out of God's lordship over everything.

We've been reflecting on the kinds of things that can be idols in our lives, such as money, possessions, success, popularity, or a certain position or title. We want these things so badly that we give all our time, resources, and energy to obtain them, thinking they will make us happy and feel secure. But when we achieve them, we find that the promises of contentment are false. The things that were shiny quickly lose their luster, and we only end up wanting more. We see it happen again and again, yet we keep falling into the same trap.

The detail that God adds to that first commandment—"Thou shalt have none other gods before me"—gives us some clue as to why this issue keeps coming up. God goes on to say, "Do not make an idol for yourself—no form whatsoever—of anything in the sky above or on the earth below or in the waters under the earth. Do not bow down to them or worship them because I, the LORD your God, am a passionate God."

The things that God lists—in the sky, on the earth, in the seas—are not inherently bad things. The Creation stories in Genesis devote a lot of detail to describing how God created them all and called them good. They're part of the created order, fashioned by God's own hand, but they're not God. They're meant to point to their maker, but we fall into idolatry when we confuse the Creation and the Creator.

The things that so frequently become idols in our own lives don't start out as inherently bad. Money is the means by which we conduct business and have access to things that meet our basic needs; it's not a bad thing at its core. The same is true of possessions, such as a place to live and clothes to wear. Succeeding in our chosen field gives us the opportunity to bless more people with our work. Friendships are fundamentally good things; God created us to be in relationship with one another. None of these things are bad in and of themselves.

The evil that comes from making idols of money and possessions isn't the stuff itself; it is found within us. We worship them because we think they are things we can have some measure of control over. Control (more accurately, the illusion of control) helps us to feel secure amid the many scary unknowns of life. It helps us feel less vulnerable. So we give our worship to different parts of the Creation, thinking that it will earn us some kind of control over it, when the whole time the "idol behind the idol" is us.

The Lord our God is unable to be controlled by anything except God's self. Resisting idolatry and worshiping God alone means giving up our illusions of control, recognizing that we are part of God's creation, and acknowledging the lordship of the Creator.

Maybe it makes sense after all to say that "I am the Lord thy God" is the first commandment.

Lord, help me to let go of my desire to posses and control. You are my Creator, and I want to worship you alone. Amen.

7. Do You Like Me?

Matthew 6:1-6, 16-18

I'm a pastor, and though the church doesn't occupy as high a place in our society as it once did, people generally respect that role. Even if they're not churchgoers, they generally assume that clergy are good people. Like most pastors, I like the esteem in other people's eyes that comes with what I do, though it's certainly not the reason I went into ordained ministry. I consider it one of the perks of the job.

We all want to be liked and respected. We want others to think we're good people, and there's nothing wrong with that. But it can become a big problem when esteem in the eyes of others goes from being a side effect to being the goal that animates all our actions.

Twentieth-century theologian Paul Tillich wrote about everyone having an "ultimate concern" in which they place all their hopes and give their best efforts. If our ultimate concern is anything less than God, it's an idol. And God is no fan of idols.

Jesus knew that one of the ways evil sneaks into our faith is that our motivation for obeying God can slowly, subtly shift from pleasing God to having others think well of us. That's why Jesus spent a good chunk of the Sermon on the Mount (his first major public teaching in the Gospel of Matthew) to pointing out the idolatry of esteem in the eyes of others.

Think about the list of things that Jesus mentions in Matthew 6: giving to the poor, praying, fasting. These are some pretty crucial things! They are all things we wouldn't do if it were only up to us. We give resources we would otherwise spend on ourselves to help people in need. We give up time we'd spend doing other things to talk with and listen to God. We intentionally deny ourselves things we enjoy, be it food or something else, so that our discomfort focuses us on God's sustaining power. But all these things that take our focus off of us can become *about* us if we're not careful. Idolatry is sneaky!

One of the weird ironies about following the liturgical calendar is that many of our churches read this passage from the Gospel of Matthew on Ash Wednesday, which begins the season of Lent. In the early church, Lent was a forty-day period of hardcore fasting when new converts would prepare themselves to be baptized before sunrise on Easter morning. In many churches, people will come to Ash Wednesday services first thing in the morning, and they will have the ashes of burned palm leaves mixed with oil smeared on their forehead in the shape of a cross and go about their day wearing those ashes.

Isn't this exactly the kind of thing Jesus warns us against doing in the Gospel passage we read in that very service? What were the people who planned the service thinking?

Perhaps they were thinking that Ash Wednesday is the most crucial time for us to be challenged to check our motivations. Going around with a big, black cross on your forehead all day is going to stand out to people, even more than someone going out in public wearing a clerical collar. So if your church uses ashes in that service, before you accept the ashes you should decide whether you're doing it so other people will think you're pious and holy, or as a reminder to yourself that you are mortal and that Jesus comes to heal your frailty.

We're especially aware of Jesus' questions and warnings on this particular day, but as people of faith they are with us every day. With every action you take, overtly religious or not, ask yourself why you're doing it and whom you're trying to please. The answer to that question will tell you where the reward will come from.

Lord, help me to serve you with my every action. If people think I'm a good person, so be it, but I want to please you first and foremost. When I lose my way, pull me back so that everything I do will be for your glory. Amen.

Week Two
MONEY, WORK, AND DEBT

⁓

8. ANOTHER KIND OF SLAVERY

Deuteronomy 28:12-14

Debt is a problem. Debt is a *big* problem. I know I'm not saying anything revolutionary, and yet debt is such a pervasive issue in our society that it bears repeating. Debt is a *huge* problem.

Debt is not a sin, thankfully, because in our world today, having some debt is almost unavoidable. Very few of us can afford to buy a house or a car outright, and there is nothing wrong with taking out a loan that we know we can pay back without too much difficulty.

The reason debt has become such a huge problem is not because it's a sin such as stealing or lying, but because we get so far behind in making our payments that we end up orienting our priorities around the debt. And, as we have learned, anything that becomes our top priority and gets our best efforts—and is not God—is an idol.

My grandfather was strongly opposed to having any kind of debt. He grew up during the Great Depression and saw many friends and neighbors lose their farms to the banks. After serving in the Navy in World War II, he worked his way through Chiropractic College and set up his practice in a small town, taking care of many farmers around the area.

There was one bank in his little town, and all the residents got their mortgages, car loans, and business loans from that bank. The president of the bank "owned" everybody in town, and he wasn't shy about reminding people of it. He could make the local government do what he wanted, was the unquestioned arbiter of all decisions in his church, and received preferential treatment everywhere he went. He got away with this because everyone owed him money. Everyone, that is, except my grandfather.

Grandpa's poor upbringing showed him how destructive debt could be, so he was very frugal. He saved all he could and only bought a new car or new equipment for his business when he had the money. He even built his house piece by piece as he was able to pay for it, out of his own pocket. My grandfather and the bank president never got along very well, because Grandpa didn't like the way the president treated people. The president resented that he didn't "own" my grandfather and his family the way he did everyone else.

When I asked Grandpa why he was so intent on avoiding debt, he said, "I was determined not to be any man's slave."

When Moses gave his farewell speech to the former Egyptian slaves whom God had liberated and led to their own land, he encouraged them to keep God's commandments for their own benefit. One of those benefits was that they would "lend to many nations, but you won't have any need to borrow" (Deuteronomy 28:12*b*). These people knew what it was to be in slavery, and they were determined not to return to it in any form, including being enslaved by debt.

Far too many of us today are enslaved by our debts to others. We get so far into debt that we orient all our priorities around keeping up with the payments, lest we get our stuff repossessed (even though we don't really need most of it to begin with). The consequences of this modern debt-slavery are many. One of the worst is that when an opportunity to participate in God's redeeming work comes along, we can't do it, because our money is spoken for before we've even earned it.

As we said last week, the first step in defeating an idol's power over us is to recognize the idol for what it is, then name it as such so we can begin to escape its slavery. May we have the courage to look at our own lives, name the debt that enslaves us, and begin taking steps to remove its shackles.

Lord, help me to make you the first priority in every area of my life. Help me to take the steps I need so that my debts do not own me and so that I am free to participate in your redeeming work in this world. Amen.

9. PKs Who Prospered

Psalm 37:21; Proverbs 22:7-9

John and Charles Wesley, the men who founded the revival movement that would come to be called Methodism and eventually become its own church, were PKs: preacher's kids. The running joke about PKs is that they either become preachers themselves or total hell-raisers. Actually, I know a couple who are both. John Wesley certainly was.

Being a pastor is hard, but it might be harder to be the family of a pastor. There's lots of pressure, the pastor is gone frequently, and the financial rewards aren't all that great. It can be a tough way to grow up. One of the reasons PKs often become preachers or hell-raisers is that, with either choice, they are trying to make sense of all they experienced in their formative years.

John and Charles Wesley saw their father Samuel Wesley go through a lot. The people in the town of Epworth, where Samuel preached, often were angry with him; more than once they may even have set his house on fire! Five-year-old John miraculously survived a house fire, and it was one of the defining experiences of his life.

But John and Charles had another formative experience that was just as important in shaping those two men and what they taught. They twice saw their father put in debtor's prison, which shamed the whole family.

In the eighteenth century, if you owed money to people and couldn't repay it, they could have you thrown in jail until you were able to pay it back. This practice raised an obvious question: How could you make money to pay back debts if you were in jail? The theory, dubious at best, must have been that your family or friends would have their arms twisted into paying your debt for you to minimize the shame.

Honor and shame were big things in the English culture of the day, and seeing their father thrown into debtor's prison must have left a huge impression on the boys. As John grew up, he kept careful account of how he spent every cent so that he would not waste anything, lest he run even the slightest risk of debt.

John Wesley's aversion to debt did not affect just his personal life. One of his most famous sermons, "The Use of Money," laid out his three rules for managing finances: earn all you can, save all you can, give all you can.

There were caveats to each rule, of course. Earning all you can doesn't honor God if you do it by dishonest means. Saving all you can shouldn't be done at the expense of your duties, such as feeding and clothing your family or tithing to the church. (Interestingly, Wesley didn't have a high opinion of leaving an inheritance for your children.) Giving all you can must be in the service of God's work in the world, to make sure that your gift is not wasted.

The subtext of Wesley's three rules on money is that following them is impossible if you find yourself enslaved to debt. You may be tempted to cut corners or do dishonest things if you are deep in debt. In today's terms, saving is next to impossible if most of your income goes to paying the interest on your credit card bill.

Likewise, the amount that you can give to the work of God is greatly diminished if your finances are tied up with debt.

The common phrase in each of these rules, *all you can*, will be different for everyone, of course. But we must ask ourselves if we are truly doing "all we can." Would it help to reduce unnecessary expenses and pay down our debts more quickly? Have we really lived to our full potential if we carry huge debts? Could our debts be overcome if we made some sacrifices for a greater good?

Lord, help me live up to the potential you have created in me. Help me make difficult decisions so I can be freer from debt and more able to serve you with all my resources. Amen.

10. LIVING AND WORKING TOGETHER

Matthew 8:21-22

Work.

It's a loaded term, if ever there was one. Saying that something is a lot of work can be an excuse to not do it. It can be a complaint or a way of emphasizing the difficulty of a task. When you ask a friend how her new job is going, she might shrug and say, "It's work," meaning it's not all that great. Social interactions often end with the phrase *I'd better get back to work*, meaning that work is an obligation.

When we talk about our work, we usually mean a job that we go to forty hours a week so we can get a paycheck and pay our bills. These days, even finding a job can be hard, and many people have had to take employment that is beneath their level of skill or training because it's better than nothing. The economy and the goal of creating jobs are frequent political talking points. But when the results aren't what was promised, we grow cynical. It's easy to understand why the term *work* often has a negative connotation. But work isn't just about punching a clock to get paid. The Bible shows us that work has a much deeper meaning and is as important to our spiritual lives as it is our economic lives.

In Genesis, God created human beings, put them in the Garden of Eden, and told them to tend it. God did not tell Adam and Eve to consume all the resources as fast as they could to maximize profit. Nor did God tell them to sit around and wait for fruit to fall from the trees so they could eat. Tending the land meant working it to help produce good things and living in harmony with it to make it fertile and useful for generations to come.

Adam and Eve were not the entitled beneficiaries of God's good creation. They were empowered to be an active part of the Lord's ongoing creative activity. We human beings, God's image bearers, were created to work—not the work of endless, meaningless toil (that part came after Adam and Eve ate the fruit and got booted out of the garden), but work that fulfills us and helps us realize the potential God created in each of us.

Work was a tricky issue in the early church, too. We read in Acts that the emerging Christian communities sold their possessions and lived together, making sure everyone had what they needed. Showing such grace carried the inherent risk that some people might take advantage of them, simply taking and not contributing to the best of their ability. So Paul and the apostles told the believers that if they did not contribute their fair share, they wouldn't be able to participate in the benefits of the communal life: "If anyone doesn't want to work, they shouldn't eat" (2 Thessalonians 3:10).

Notice the phrase *want to*. There were undoubtedly some in these communities, just as there are today, who were limited in their ability to work, or just plain unable. Someone who had lost both legs wouldn't be left out because of inability to work the fields. People who were unable to work were taken care of, and they made contributions in other ways.

The early church was able to act fairly because of the mutual love and trust that existed among its members, and because the network of relationships was strong enough that people knew one another's abilities. They loved each other enough to hold each other accountable for doing their fair share of the work, whatever that fair share was.

Our work is an essential part of being the people God created us to be. It is a crucial part of our lives of faith, because we fully experience the blessings of community when we give all that we can to its common life. Our lives are not full without work!

God, thank you for work. Thank you for giving each of us different abilities and showing us how to work together to achieve your purposes. Help me work as hard as I can and give my best effort so I can be an instrument of your blessing to others. Amen.

11. About the Quick Fix

Proverbs 14:23; 12:11

Patience is a virtue.

Waiting is no fun.

Both of these statements are true. They always have been, but perhaps the tension between them has never been as great as it is in our world today. Think about it: almost every advertisement or mass media message has instant gratification as its subtext. Hungry? Why wait? Buy this meal you can microwave in seconds, or hit the drive-through where we'll have a clock literally counting the seconds it takes us to serve you. If your football team's high draft pick isn't dominating the league from day one, he's considered a bust. If an elected official doesn't change the entire political culture as soon as she sets foot in the legislature, we're upset with her.

It once took letters weeks or more to travel great distances. Now we can text or email each another instantly. Want to lose weight? Try this miracle product that will help you do it without diet or exercise. Oh, and here's a get-rich-quick scheme with zero risk and minimal effort required.

Ideally, the church would be the place where we stand against this cultural tide of instant gratification, but church members are human and fall to this temptation, too. Business thrives on the idea of quick spiritual transformation with very little effort. Pastors and church staff eagerly grab the latest book or product with the hopes that it will quickly turn their ministries around.

In each of these examples, we are disappointed when we fail to receive instantaneous results, so we go searching for the next thing making big promises. And the self-defeating cycle continues.

But the witness of the Bible is that instant gratification is not the answer. Twice Proverbs mentions the value of working hard day after day to build something that lasts, contrasting that hard, faithful work with those seeking quick results.

One of the best things my parents taught me growing up was the value of patience and hard work, but those lessons didn't come from speeches or sermons. They came from having a garden. In a corner of our backyard was a small patch of ground that was tilled up where we would plant lettuce, tomatoes, cucumbers, and other vegetables. We planted early in the spring, and we waited. Every couple of days we would have to go out and pull weeds that were taking precious nutrients from our vegetables, and deal with any bugs or other critters that wanted a quick snack.

We didn't get to enjoy the fruits of our labor (well, technically the only fruit was the tomato) for weeks or even months, but when we did, they tasted great. In contrast to the mass-produced greenhouse vegetables from the grocery store, these actually had flavor! We learned that our hard work and patience made for a better result than what we could get quickly with minimal effort.

In virtually every area of life, real and lasting good doesn't come quickly. We lose weight and become healthier by developing better habits that we can sustain over a lifetime. The money from a get-rich-quick scheme disappears as fast as it shows up. Our relationships with family and friends become healthy because we regularly dedicate time and energy to them, dealing openly and honestly with conflicts when they come along instead of avoiding discomfort by pretending they're not there.

Our relationship with God is the same way. We may have a dramatic conversion such as the apostle Paul had, or we might experience a spiritual high in a worship service or on a mission trip. But to achieve lasting quality in that relationship, we must regularly set aside time to pray, study the Scriptures, and make the journey of faith with others.

Patience and hard work may not be fun, but the result is much more satisfying than that of the quick and easy path.

Lord, the world I live in tells me that instant results are the best. Help me to sow good things and tend to them, and be patient for lasting results. Give me strength for the long journey, and fill me with faith in your promise of great reward. Amen.

12. Empty Words

Matthew 21:28-31

Around the time of the 2008 financial crisis, it was discovered that a guy named Bernie Madoff, considered to be a financial wizard, had been running a "Ponzi scheme" for years. He had taken millions of dollars from people, saying he would invest it, but instead he kept it for himself. Madoff carried the ruse on for years by producing documents that convinced his clients they were making money. When finally he was caught, people were amazed that he had been able to run the scam for so long with no one suspecting. After all, some of his clients were among the richest people in the world, and they didn't get that way by being dumb with their money or naively trusting the wrong people. Bernie Madoff was able to talk a very good game, but when the results came to light, everyone found out that all his talk was just that: talk. Empty words, nothing more.

We do a lot of talking in religious circles. It's fairly easy to stand up in front of people and paint yourself as a devout, hardworking person whose example should be followed by everyone else—witness all the preachers and politicians who have been caught doing things that didn't match up with their public image.

The problem is nothing new, of course. Jesus butted heads with the religious establishment of his day, calling them out on their hypocrisy. When he taught at the Temple in Jerusalem, the chief priests and elders became upset. This was their turf! Who did this uneducated country preacher think he was? By what authority did he teach? They asked Jesus that very question in an attempt to trap him. Jesus didn't fall for it, though. He lobbed the question right back at them, asking them by what authority John the Baptist taught. They said they didn't know, and the conversation was over.

But Jesus didn't stop there. He told a parable about two sons whose father told them to go work in the vineyard. One said no but ended up working. The other said yes but, in effect, stayed home and played video games all day. Jesus was not so subtly implying that the powerful men who ran the religious establishment were the ones who said *yes* to God for everyone to hear, but whose actions didn't back up their words. Jesus taught that the important thing wasn't words but doing God's will.

When your church has a stewardship program, you focus on giving as part of your journey of discipleship. You probably are asked to make a financial pledge for the coming year, and you might even be encouraged to talk openly in your small group, your Sunday school class, or circle of friends about what you will pledge.

This openness can be a good thing, because in our culture we tend to keep our financial lives very private, thus cutting off intimate parts of our lives from those with whom we are supposed to be completely honest. I hope that you have a group of people you can turn to in discussing these parts of your life and that you can encourage and challenge one another to deepen your journey of discipleship through financial giving.

The temptation you will encounter—and you may already see someone who has fallen into it—is to talk about giving but not to back up the words with actions. If you can make a generous step in faith and share that as an example to others, God bless you for it. But consider that Jesus might rather you be a faithful, secret giver. In either case, whatever you give, do it for the glory of God alone.

Lord, help me give unselfishly. I want the glory to belong to you, not me. Help my actions match my words so that your kingdom will be strengthened. Amen.

13. SEVENTY TIMES SEVEN

Matthew 18:21-35 (NRSV)

Steve and Joe had been best friends all their lives. They met in elementary school and went to the same church. When they grew up, Steve was in the worship band, and Joe was a Sunday school teacher. People looked to them as examples of what good Christian men are supposed to be. Even though they had jobs and families, Steve and Joe still met for coffee each week to talk honestly about their lives, encourage one another in areas where they were struggling, and pray together.

One week, Steve got so caught up with a project at work that he lost track of the time and not only missed his coffee appointment with Joe but didn't even text Joe to say he wouldn't be able to come. Joe sat at the coffee shop for a while before going home, annoyed and a little mad.

The next day Steve called Joe to apologize, and he was shocked at Joe's reply: "I don't forgive you. I don't have to. This is the 491st time you've messed up, and I've already forgiven you the exact number of times the Bible says I have to." (In some translations of today's Scripture, Jesus tells Peter to forgive his brother "seventy times seven" or 490 times.)

Steve couldn't believe what he was hearing! Joe began to list some of the 490 times Steve had messed up, starting with calling him a "doo-doo head" on the playground when they were six. Joe went on to say, "This is offense number 491, and according to Matthew 18, you've used up all the times I have to forgive you. It's in the Bible, bro."

Steve thought about it for a minute, then asked, "Joe, if you've spent the last twenty years keeping a mental count of every time I've messed up (and for the record, I don't think you're a doo-doo head), then did you really forgive me for any of those things in the first place?"

Forgiveness is a tough thing. We trust in God's complete forgiveness of all our sins, but for most of us it's hard to let go of old grudges against other people. Most people apologize for what they did, but what about those who aren't sorry and would never consider apologizing because they believe what they did was right?

Jesus tells us that we won't truly experience forgiven unless we let go of the hurt that others have caused us and extend forgiveness to them. It's one thing to forgive somebody who missed a coffee appointment, but what about the person who sexually assaulted a friend or killed a family member in a drunk-driving accident? Is it possible for us to forgive so that when we think of that person, we won't remember the hurtful actions but instead will see someone made in God's image?

If we rely solely on our own strength, the answer probably is no. We won't be able to let those things go and forgive even if we want to. Some wounds are so deep that we need outside help in healing them. Left to our own devices, we'll be like the unforgiving servant in Jesus' parable. We'll be happy that someone was nice and let us off the hook for something we did wrong, but when it's our turn we'll be so selfish that it will be clear we haven't understood what it means to be truly forgiven.

That's why we look to God for the strength to let these things go and begin the journey of forgiveness. We ask for that strength whenever we pray the Lord's Prayer together, asking God to forgive our sins in the same measure as we forgive those who sin against us.

Does someone owe you a debt? Whether it's an amount of money or restitution for a physical or emotional wound, ask God for the strength to forgive. When you do, you will begin to learn what it is to be truly, deeply forgiven.

Lord, I have received your forgiveness, but it's hard for me to forgive others. Help me to forgive as you forgive. Help me to see others as you see them: not as sinners, but as your children in need of redemption. Amen.

14. GOD'S RESET BUTTON

Deuteronomy 15:1

In the Torah, the people of Israel were commanded to practice jubilee. Every seven years, all debts were forgiven and indentured servants were allowed to return to their families. Every fiftieth year (the end of seven of these cycles of seven years each), there would be a time of "jubilee," when fields would lie fallow and land would be returned to its original owners. You might say it was a time when God pushed the reset button.

Imagine what would happen today if we practiced jubilee. Student loans would be forgiven. We could live without fear that missing one mortgage payment would ruin us, or that one major health crisis would put us on the street. We could live with more freedom in our lives, because the burden of our past wouldn't be an albatross around our neck.

Of course, some people would object, saying that jubilee would encourage people to be irresponsible. After all, if every debt were forgiven, why worry about repaying anyone? In addition, people who had money might stop lending because there would be no guarantee of getting repaid. The economy would grind to a halt!

All that may be true, but the purpose of jubilee is not to excuse people from being responsible. The point is to create justice.

If we trusted that our debts would be forgiven and wanted to use that forgiveness responsibly, then perhaps we would make sure not to incur debts that we wouldn't be able to pay back. Besides encouraging responsible borrowing, jubilee might discourage irresponsible lending. Predatory lenders who offer loans that people can't repay wouldn't be able to engage in that practice, because they would have to forgive the loan at a set date.

Another feature of jubilee was that slaves would be set free every seventh year. This made sense in the ancient world, because people often had to enter indentured servitude to pay a debt. Today, excessive debts create a very different kind of enslavement that overwhelms people's lives for decades, sometimes with no end in sight. God's wants us to live responsibly, so that the only contract that lasts is our covenant relationship with him.

The ultimate lesson of jubilee is about forgiveness. Forgiveness is not something that happens just because we're feeling charitable that day or because the debtor has repented. Forgiveness isn't earned at all. It's given as God's free gift, because God values relationships more than repayment.

There may not be anyone who owes you money, but you might have a relationship that remains strained because of a past sin or conflict. If that's true, then it's time to practice jubilee and let it go. It's time to push the reset button on our lives, to open ourselves to new opportunities, to start with a clean slate and do better this time around.

Lord, help me to forgive even when I don't feel like forgiving. Give me the strength to trust in the promise of jubilee and live responsibly so that I will not be enslaved to anything. Help me to live my life with a clean slate and enable others to do so, too. Amen.

Be Faithful, Save, and Give

⌒

15. A Tale of Two Churches

2 Corinthians 8:1-9, 9:5-6

By the time Paul wrote 2 Corinthians, he had been traveling, preaching, and starting new faith communities for a long time, so he'd had the opportunity to see how churches reacted to different circumstances. Some churches endured hardships from day one. Maybe they had been persecuted by local authorities that wanted them to acknowledge the lordship of Caesar. Maybe their town was in the midst of an economic downturn, and the members had a hard time caring for one another. Other churches seemed to have it easy, maybe too easy, for trials and hardship can deepen and strengthen faith.

As different as the experiences of these early churches were, nearly all of them had one thing in common. They were cheerful and generous givers to the work of churches outside their own city.

In today's Scripture, Paul was writing to the Corinthians about the church in Macedonia, which was just north of Greece, where

Corinth was located. The churches in Macedonia and Corinth provided a study in contrasts. While the Macedonian church experienced persecution and hardship, Corinth was a wealthy, diverse city where many citizens, including people in the church, lived quite comfortably. Read 1 Corinthians if you want to know more about how too much comfort can lead to problems such as idolatry and infighting.

In spite of the differences between the churches at Macedonia and Corinth, Paul bragged to each church about the other's generosity of spirit. Was Paul stoking the churches' pride, trying to get them to one-up each other? Maybe, but it was for the cause of spreading the gospel.

We don't know the dollar amounts of the offerings given by the Macedonian and Corinthian churches, but we can make an educated guess that the Corinthians gave a lot more, since they were generally a wealthier church. Just because Corinth could put a bigger check in the plate, however, didn't mean that their offering was better. As a matter of fact, Paul suggested that the Macedonians' offering might be greater in God's eyes, because they gave a greater percentage of what they had.

Paul reminded the Corinthians that "the one who sows a small number of seeds will also reap a small crop, and the one who sows a generous amount of seeds will also reap a generous crop." These are terms we can understand. "Small" and "generous" were respective portions of what each church gave, and those portions say something significant about the spiritual life of the Corinthian community.

Paul was echoing something Jesus taught his disciples. In Mark 12:41-44, Jesus observed people bringing gifts to the Temple. While some people gave large amounts of money, a poor widow put two small coins in the collection box. Jesus said that her gift was worth more because she wasn't just giving extra, disposable income. The widow could barely afford to feed herself, but she knew she had an obligation as one of God's children to give to the common good.

In my denomination, The United Methodist Church, every congregation is supposed to give a certain amount of money every year to the work of the larger church. These gifts are called apportionments, and bigger congregations with more resources are asked to contribute more than smaller congregations. As you might imagine, some people don't like the idea of apportionments. Some see it as nothing more than a kind of tax that takes away from their congregation's ability to minister to its community. It's true that some apportioned funds are spent less wisely than others, but pooling our money together funds mission efforts that no church could accomplish on its own, such as supporting universities, seminaries, and disaster relief work around the world.

It's amazing to see how a congregation's spiritual health is mirrored by the extent to which it gives to causes outside itself. Churches that pay all their apportionments, or as much as they are able, have a much greater sense of connection with the larger body of Christ. Those that give generously, especially those that give beyond what seems to be their ability, realize it's not all about them. It's about something bigger than we are, and the more we participate, the greater sense of satisfaction we experience in the work of the whole.

What is true for congregations is also true for individuals. When we step outside ourselves and give generously, when we fully participate in something bigger than we are, we experience the blessing of accomplishing things together.

Lord, help me to sow generously, so that I may experience the blessing of the great crop we will all reap together. Help me to step outside myself and be part of this great body that you have created us to be. Amen.

16. What's in Your Heart?

2 Corinthians 9:7

Our family just became involved in the ministry of foster care. It was the end result of several years of prayerful discernment that included having a second child and buying a house. It was something we had talked about from time to time, but as a "one day" sort of thing. My wife and I are in our thirties, and our kids are young, plus we're both working hard to become more established in our respective careers. But God kept tugging on my wife's heart. Eventually she talked me into attending a certification class, because it wouldn't obligate us to anything.

I'm pretty sure that at the class meetings I wore my skepticism on my sleeve. It was several hours one evening each week, after I'd already worked a very long day. I wasn't exactly cheerful about participating, much less welcoming another child into our home. I could articulate a hundred reasons not to do it. But from my own journey as a pastor, I know that God's call on our lives is sometimes strongest when we feel pulled toward something even as we want to run the other way.

Over the weeks, we heard lots of stories from people who had been involved in foster care. Some of the stories were about children with serious behavioral issues and biological parents with violent tendencies. And yet, even while they were telling stories that made the logical part of my brain want to get up and walk out, something kept me glued to my seat. Maybe it was God calling our family to this ministry. Maybe it was the absolute joy on the faces of the foster parents, even as they were telling stories of tragedy and heartbreak.

We had chances to talk with our classmates about why they were there. Some people were looking to adopt children. Some talked in religious terms as we did, while others did not. One commonality was the sense that they had something they wanted to share with someone who needed it. They were compelled by something deep within them, just as my wife was (and eventually I was), to give not out of obligation, but out of love and joy.

Paul talks about our motivations for giving. He says, in essence, that it's gut-check time. Don't give just because you see other people around you doing it, or because you think you're supposed to. Tithing ten percent of your income is great, but God is much more concerned about what is in your heart.

So, what's in yours? What is God leading you to give? Sharing your finances is part of it, certainly. After all, we are the only bank account God has, and the church needs funds to do the work God has called us to do. But where is your heart in this? What stokes your passions? What things get you riled up or even upset enough to make you say, "Someone should do something about this"?

That someone might be you. God may be tugging on your heart to give in a new way that you hadn't previously considered. What kind of giving brings you joy? It is there that you will begin to discover the ways God wants to use you.

Lord, help me to know what you want me to give. Put the desire in my heart to share the blessings you have given me. Let me give with joy so that others will see your spirit in me. Amen.

17. ABUNDANCE

2 Corinthians 9:8-9; Philippians 4:19; Matthew 7:7-11

Occasionally when I'm flipping channels on the TV, I come across a Christian station whose programming might be described as a little over-the-top. I'm a fairly formal, high-church Methodist, so seeing people with the big hair, the loud clothes, and the yelling and jumping is both strange and fascinating to me. I have friends who practice a charismatic style of faith, and I've enjoyed attending services with them, but these TV shows take it to a new level.

Cultural and stylistic differences aside, I do have disagreements with what I see on some of the shows. The preachers ask you to give money, promising that God will make you wealthy in return. I guess I've seen one too many news stories on the subject, but it seems to me that the only people getting rich are the preachers, not the viewers. I start getting upset, so I have to turn off the TV for the good of my soul.

What these folks are preaching has a couple of different names, but most people know it as the prosperity gospel. The idea is that God rewards your generosity, especially if you give in amounts you can't afford, by showering you with riches. Many Christians in mainline denominations have written these preachers off. As a result, some of us have started shying away from talking about money at all, so that folks won't lump us together with the folks we see on TV.

The problem is that, in fact, the Bible talks a lot about money and material possessions. The Bible talks a lot about faithful giving, and there are quite a few Scriptures where we are told that God will provide for all our needs. How do we take these Scriptures seriously when we see TV preachers getting obscenely rich while tens of thousands of children starve to death every day? How are we to be faithful to this part of God's word?

It helps us to distinguish between extravagance and abundance. Extravagance is excessive, more than what is really necessary. It's difficult for us to justify extravagance in material possessions when we know that God has called us to share our resources and care for a hurting world.

But abundance is different. The abundance described in the Gospels and the letters of Paul is not excessive or more than necessary. The abundance of God fills us at our deepest level and satisfies a hunger that no meal, no matter how extravagant, can touch. According to Paul, God grants us abundance not so we can keep what we are given, but so we will have "more than enough for every kind of good work." Abundance equips us to participate in God's redeeming work in the world, not simply to further the inequality we see all around us.

We experience abundance most fully when we open ourselves to God. When we do so, God plants in us a generosity of spirit that will lead us to provide resources for God's work in the world, not just for our own material comforts. God may not give us every single thing we want, but if we are patient, what we truly need will never be far away.

Lord, help me to know what to ask you for, and give me the faith to know that you will provide it. Lead me to look out not for my own personal desires, but for ways you can use me to bless others. Amen.

18. A Crop of Righteousness

2 Corinthians 9:10-12; Psalm 139:14

What does it mean to believe that God will supply us with everything we need? It's hard to reconcile our faith in this promise with the reality of a world in which the vast majority of resources are controlled by a very few people. If I'm happy and comfortable, it's easy for me to say that God is providing. But what about the people down the street or halfway around the world who don't know where their next meal is coming from or when it will be? How can I say that God is providing for them when they have so many needs that clearly go unmet?

Paul shines some light on these questions. He writes that God will "multiply your seed and increase your crop, *which is righteousness*" (emphasis added). Could it be that the crop God wants us to produce isn't primarily a physical thing? The seeds that God provides and calls us to care for will produce a crop not of corn or wheat, but of righteousness.

What does it mean to produce a crop of righteousness? As the psalmist says, each of us is wonderfully and fearfully made— unique, with our own gifts and graces to use in accomplishing God's purposes in the world. God knows us better than we know ourselves, so we trust in God's leading to show us how to use what he has given us.

Most of us reading this book are among the wealthiest people in the world. We consume more than our share of the world's resources on a daily basis. We may not have created this inequality, but the way we live our lives certainly perpetuates it.

So, for those of us living in Western society, perhaps the crop of righteousness means shifting the way we use the resources at our disposal. What would it mean to consume less and save more, so we could give the extra to those who need it? It may be that God's way of providing for the needs of the world is, quite simply, us.

Several families in one affluent church found themselves becoming dissatisfied with the way they and their neighbors were defining success: making more money, buying a bigger house, driving a fancier car. They were searching for success, but the satisfaction they sought never came, and they wondered if it ever would.

Eventually the families chose to live more simply. They moved into smaller houses, downsized to one car per family, and shared meals several times a week so they would waste less food. They kept making the same amounts of money, but all of a sudden they had many more resources to share. After the first year they had saved enough money to dig over a dozen wells in Africa, and a year later they decided to go see first-hand what their giving had accomplished. When the families saw a village thriving because of the clean water they had provided, they finally felt the peace and satisfaction they had been chasing all those years.

The families' "crop of righteousness" came about because they considered the resources at their disposal and discerned how God wanted to use those resources to bless others. These became the seeds that produced a crop halfway around the world.

What about you? What resources in your life might become seeds to grow a crop of righteousness? When you see the seeds, don't hesitate to tend them. God is using you to plant and harvest an incredible crop.

Lord, help me see the seeds you have placed in my life. Give me the wisdom and courage to use them in accordance with your will. Help me to trust in your promise that the crop of righteousness you produce in me will bring greater joy than any material possession. Amen.

19. Be Prepared

Genesis 41:17-38; Proverbs 21:20; 27:23-27

You have to admire Joseph. The guy kept being knocked down and getting back up for more. He was like an ancient Rocky Balboa (from the first two movies, not the final three).

Joseph was the youngest son in his family and the favorite, and he made sure his brothers knew it. He pushed them so far that finally they sold him into slavery and told their father that Joseph had died. But Joseph was a survivor. Eventually he landed a decent job in a nice house in Egypt, only to be thrown in jail on false charges when he refused to have an affair with his boss's wife. Joseph made a friend in prison who promised to help get him out, but the plan took two years.

Finally Joseph's luck turned. He had a gift for predicting the future by interpreting dreams and was given a chance to read the dreams of the Pharaoh. Joseph told the Pharaoh there will be seven years of plenty, followed by seven years of famine, so the Egyptian people had better get smart and save up during the good years. Joseph's wisdom and foresight won him the job of prime minister, answering only to Pharaoh himself.

The Bible doesn't tell us, but the reaction among the people in Egypt must have been interesting. If there had been newspaper editorials or cable news channels at the time, there might have been harsh criticism. Who was this foreigner who had come out of nowhere and was running the whole show? There would have been allegations about his past with the boss's wife. Why was Joseph holding all of the surplus back? Shouldn't hard-working Egyptians be rewarded for their seven years of bountiful harvest?

Human beings are notoriously shortsighted. Even if the people had known about Joseph's prophecy of a coming famine, would they have believed him? They might have wanted to throw big, lavish parties using all the surplus and not worry about saving for hard times. After all, how bad could it be? Was the rain just going to stop falling?

Well, yes, it did. The famine devastated communities across the ancient Near East, but Egypt had the means not only to feed its own people but people from other nations, because Joseph had saved for a time when things got tough.

The recent economic crisis in the United States showed us the consequences of assuming that good times would never end. Real estate speculation ran rampant because people assumed that values would just keep going up. But then the bubble burst, and a lot of people looked foolish because they had no backup plan.

Adjustable-rate mortgages that had looked like such a good deal suddenly had their rates jacked up, and people found themselves owing more on their houses than the properties were worth. People lost their jobs and couldn't handle the massive debt.

In Proverbs, the wise teacher instructs us to plan ahead, "for no treasure lasts forever." There will be lean years and years of plenty. Sometimes we know when those years will come, but most of the time we don't. Circumstances can change quickly, so we must be prepared. As in the Great Depression of the 1930s, those who weathered the storm were the ones who had realized the good times wouldn't last and had planned accordingly.

What would happen if you lost your job next week? Do you have enough on hand to meet your obligations for at least a few months? Or would you be caught in a bind because you'd been living beyond your means?

If the latter describes your situation, prayerfully consider talking to a financial professional or a knowledgeable friend to find out ways to save for the future. The only constant is change, so be prepared when it comes.

Lord, help me to be wise and save for difficult times. I want to be a blessing to others during hard days, not a burden. Let my example be a witness to others of faithful living. Amen.

20. Rich Toward God

Luke 12:16-21

Being prudent and saving for a rainy day are good things. In fact, they're things that are encouraged in a number of different places in the Bible. But like any good thing, this strategy can be pushed too far. At what point does being smart and saving for the future turn into selfishness? What is the proper balance between saving and giving?

Though there is no hard-and-fast answer, Jesus told a story that gives us guidance. A landowner had an excellent harvest. The harvest was so plentiful that he didn't have enough room to store it all! So he decided to build bigger barns to store his crop so he could survive on the surplus for several years.

This seems like a smart decision, right? But Jesus said that God was upset with the man, because if he died that night, all of his surplus would go to waste. The parable probably sounded strange to a first-century audience, and it sounds even stranger today. The man should have been a hero, right? He had every right to make a profit from his plentiful harvest. What exactly did he do wrong?

Verse 19 provides a clue. When the landowner was making these plans, he decided to rest on his laurels: "I'll say to myself, you have stored up plenty of goods, enough for several years. Take it easy! Eat, drink, and enjoy yourself!" But the plentiful harvest had given him far more than he needed, so he had the chance to do some incredible things with it. He squandered the chance, opting instead to celebrate, because he thought he had earned it.

What would have happened if, instead of storing up the surplus, the man had imagined possibilities for sharing the blessing? He could have put some of the crop aside to have good seeds for the following season. He could have taken the profits from selling those extra crops and given ten percent or more to the work of God. That would have been a good start.

But what should the man have done then? He was wealthy, comfortable, and successful, so we can assume he was used to setting goals and working toward them. What would have come next? One possibility would have been to reward those who had helped produce the bountiful harvest. After all, there was no way he could reap such a big crop all by himself. He had laborers to do the work in the fields. He could reward them for their good work with a nice bonus. He could also look around his community and see who was struggling to make it from one day to the next. He might realize that he had an opportunity to make their lives easier through a generous gift.

At the end of the day, the man would only get so much satisfaction out of eating, drinking, and taking it easy. He will get hungry again and might have a hangover from too much partying. The satisfaction he would get from sharing his bountiful harvest would last far longer than the enjoyment of a good meal and a nice bottle of wine. He might sleep more soundly, knowing he had made his neighbors' lives easier and that God had used him to make his corner of the world a better place. He could be filled with joy, because his faith had led him to save wisely and give generously, to be "rich toward God."

God, help me to know how much is enough. I want to be rich toward you, not toward myself. Show me how to share my blessings so that all your children will benefit from the gifts you have given me. May I glorify you in all that I do. Amen.

21. Just a Little Bit More

Psalm 50:10; Mark 6:34-43

How do we define *enough*? When do we know that we have achieved enough social status, enough economic security, or enough anything else? How do we know when we get there?

Several studies have been done in which researchers have asked people at various salary levels if they felt happy and secure, and if not, what it would take for them to feel that way. Amazingly, virtually all people across the spectrum, from millionaires to those scraping by on minimum wage, said that if they were making about ten percent more, they would be satisfied—nothing outlandish, mind you. Just a little bit more would be enough, and then they could finally relax.

That nearly universal desire for "just a little bit more" shows that most of us live with a theology of scarcity. We may not necessarily express it in religious terms, but our default is to see the inherently limited nature of the resources out there and begin to figure out how we can get our slice of them. We have to look out for number one, because if we don't, no one will.

This view of scarcity is not entirely our fault: It's in the air. Politicians try to win our votes by telling us their policies will get us more. Companies want to help us refinance our mortgages, consolidate our debts, and make our investments turn a quick profit. Why? Because that's the way that we'll get that "just a little bit more" and finally be satisfied. That is, until you get used to having that much, and you want another ten percent.

God's promises stand in stark contrast to the theology of scarcity. The Psalms were written at a time when a system of sacrifices was still in place, and people worried about whether they had made the proper offering. Some people probably thought if they were able to give "just a little bit more," then maybe God would finally be pleased with them.

But what people forgot—and what we forget when we assume that our efforts are somehow "enough" for God—is that everything belongs to God. God was never going to look down from the clouds and say, "Wow, Joe gave all those bulls. I really needed that! What a great guy Joe is!" The bulls were God's to begin with. Joe's offering to God is either a cheap trick to buy favor, or an expression of gratitude for what God has already done.

To Jesus, a "meager" offering was actually more than enough to accomplish a miracle. In Mark's version of today's story, the five loaves and two fish were all the disciples had with them. In other Gospels, the food belongs to a young boy who selflessly gives them to Jesus, not knowing if he'll get a single bite. This kid was not looking out for number one! But as small as his offering was, Jesus multiplied it, giving people more than enough to eat and having twelve baskets left over.

Some people wonder whether Jesus' miracle was supernatural in nature, with the fish and bread materializing out of thin air, or if the selfless gift inspired others in the crowd to share what they had, even if it was not much. Maybe the miracle was that the people's hearts turned from a theology of scarcity to a theology of abundance. They learned that God will provide more than we need if we are willing to risk sharing what we do have, even when it seems like "not enough."

Whichever explanation of the miracle you like better, the truth proclaimed by this story is the same. Jesus multiplies what is faithfully given, when nothing is held back because we're worried about having "enough" or chasing after "just a little bit more."

May we allow God to open our hearts to a theology of abundance in this season of giving.

Lord, help me share what I have, even when I feel that it's not enough. Help me trust in your provision and look for the good of others before my own good. Amen.

Week Four

HEART GIVING

22. DIFFERENT BUT THE SAME

Matthew 6:33

One of my favorite praise choruses growing up in church was this one: "Seek ye first the Kingdom of God and his righteousness, and all these things shall be added unto you, allelu, alleluia."[1] To a kid in an affluent suburb, those lyrics were a reminder that though much of the culture around us is focused on gaining more and getting ahead, our priority as followers of Jesus is to seek God's will before our own material good. A song can do more to teach theology than a sermon or Bible study. Having that simple chorus in my head helped me navigate a social scene in which people's worth was measured by what cars they drove, what clothes they wore, how attractive they were, and how good they were at sports.

As I grew older and learned more about the world of the Bible, I realized that the Sermon on the Mount was preached not to affluent suburban kids but to poor people who had to work hard every day just to survive. "Do not worry about what you wear" sounds very different to someone struggling to find or make clothes than it does to someone concerned about which label is on the clothes. "Do not worry about what you will eat" has a very different meaning to someone who wonders where the next meal will come from than it does to someone whose biggest food worry is which cookies are in the pantry.

Not all of us live in affluent suburbs, but for most of us, our experience of having the basic necessities of life, such as food and clothes, is a lot closer to the modern suburban teenager than the first-century Palestinian peasant. Given the radical differences between those two life experiences, we have to ask what, if anything, this part of the Sermon on the Mount says to us today.

Recognizing such cultural differences is an essential part of understanding some deeper meanings in the biblical texts, but those differences don't have to be a barrier. True, there is much that a person who lived during Jesus' time wouldn't recognize about our lives today, and vice versa. But at our core there are some basic things about human beings that transcend time, culture, and economic status. Jesus' central message in this part of the Sermon on the Mount is about worry and our orientation toward physical possessions, and all humans deal with that no matter who we are.

Someone who runs a small business in the United States today might not have to worry about where the next meal is coming from, but there is still plenty to worry about. The person needs enough money in the bank to make payroll, must save enough for retirement and the kids' college, and must deal with the family's mortgage and bills. The business owner may not worry about starving tomorrow, but the prospect of going out of business is very real.

Regarding the material things in our lives, Jesus tells us to remember that these things may be important, but they're not ultimate. Take the long view, he tells us. In the final analysis, God is not going to judge you or me on how much money we made or whether our business succeeded.

In the daily pursuits of life, how do you see yourself participating in the work of God's kingdom? You don't need to have a church vocation to do that. As a matter of fact, you might be able to do more good outside the institutional church! How are you honoring God in the way you make money and provide for your family? Are you working to share your means with those who legitimately must worry about where their next meal is coming from? When we place our highest priority on serving God and furthering the work of the Kingdom, the other worries don't go away. But in the light of eternity, suddenly they don't seem like such a big deal.

Lord, help me to seek you first. Help me to trust that you will guide me in all my responsibilities, and that all the other things will fall into place when my highest priority is you. Amen.

---

1. Karen Lafferty, "Seek Ye First," *The United Methodist Hymnal* (Nashville: The United Methodist Publishing House, 1989), 405.

23. Grace Isn't Fair

Leviticus 19:9-10; Luke 4:23-30

In the United States today, there is a lot of talk about immigration. According to one recent estimate, there are about eleven million people in the United States who have immigrated illegally, their status being undocumented. Every campaign season, candidates boast about how tough they will be on illegal immigration. Rarely do any of these people know an undocumented immigrant personally, nor do they know the stories of those who make the choice to break a law in search of a better life for themselves and their families.

Whatever our opinions about laws and policies, beneath all the immigration rhetoric are human beings, most of whom live on the margins of society, working hard and often living in fear of those outside of their own communities.

The question of how to deal with foreigners in one's own land is a very old one. God addressed it in the laws of Moses, where he commanded the people to look past national identities with compassion for all human beings.

When Israelites were harvesting grain from their fields or grapes from their vineyard, they were supposed to leave "gleanings" (extra crops) around the edges. In addition, whatever fell to the ground before farmers came through and harvested themselves was to be left there, so that "the poor and the immigrant" could have them.

At first glance, this seems unfair. Every grape, every grain of wheat was the owner's property. That owner worked hard to produce a good crop and deserved to be rewarded by making as much profit as he could. It hardly seems fair that property owners had to leave some of the crop for people who didn't share in the labor.

But grace isn't fair. It isn't fair that God took human form to redeem us in the midst of our stubborn rebellion. It isn't fair that we keep being forgiven when our actions don't merit forgiveness. Grace challenges our understanding of what "fair" really is.

Let's also remember who the Israelites were. They were not the original inhabitants of that land. Every field and vineyard was once owned by someone else. The Israelites were there because God had empowered them to conquer and possess the land. They too had been foreigners in a strange land, and the God who delivered them commanded them to care for those who were far from home and quite likely experiencing the kind of hardship the Israelites knew only too well. God had shown compassion and love for them in their time of need, so God was telling them to remember that when they found themselves on the other side of the equation.

But humans are shortsighted and tend to forget. Just as most Americans forget that their ancestors were immigrants, most of whom had no legal right to come, the Israelites forgot this too.

Grace isn't fair. It never has been and never will be. Whether it's leaving gleanings in your fields so the poor and the immigrants can have something to eat; whether it's realizing that in God's eyes there are no favorites; whether it's looking past labels such as *illegal* and seeing fellow human beings in need, grace isn't fair. God gave us grace when we didn't deserve it, and we are called to pass that grace on to others, whether we think they deserve it or not.

Lord, help me to look past people's differences and see brothers and sisters who each bear your image. Help me to give generously to those in need, whether I think they deserve it or not. Let me be so full of unfair grace that I spread it to whomever I encounter. Amen.

24. A WARM WELCOME

Matthew 25:35-36; Proverbs 19:17; James 1:27

Our church participates in a ministry called Room in the Inn, in which homeless people sleep in different churches each night of the week during the winter. We welcome ten men each Wednesday night, which coincides with our Wednesday night dinner and programming. We like to think we're hospitable, because we eat at the same table with our homeless brothers, and we serve them a multi-course meal on real china with real silverware. This is a ministry that many people in our congregation actively support, but there is a danger in getting too proud of ourselves.

A few weeks before the Room in the Inn season started, we brought a new pastor onto our staff. She had many different areas of responsibility. The greatest blessing she brought was a set of fresh eyes to see things we may have taken for granted. She had the courage to challenge us to do better.

The new pastor took one look at the area where we welcomed our homeless guests and said, "This is completely unacceptable." What? How could that be? We went out of our way to welcome these guests and set up an area just for this ministry. What on earth did she mean?

The third-floor area in question had had many different uses over the years, but in recent times it had become a storage area for miscellaneous items. Stereo equipment, clothes, furniture—all ended up on the third floor. Out of sight, out of mind.

The problem was that because we didn't often think about how the area appeared to other people, we missed the message the clutter was saying to our guests, "Here, sleep in our junk. Aren't we generous?"

Rarely does the Bible get specific about how we are to be judged, but Matthew 25 gives us a clue. In that Scripture, the difference between the sheep and the goats has nothing to do with our beliefs, with our positions on social issues, or what translation of the Bible we read. It has everything to do with how we treat those to whom the world tells us we owe nothing. Those who are considered "the least of these" by everyone else are precious in the eyes of God, and failing to care for them is not an option.

Proverbs 19:17 tells us, "Those who are gracious to the poor lend to the LORD, and the Lord will fully repay them." In God's kingdom, no one gets left out. So the question is, how fully are we willing to live out the reality of the Kingdom in a world that plays by a different set of rules? How fully do we commit to the promise that those who are deemed "lazy" or "takers" are actually of supreme worth in the eyes of God?

James, a disciple who could not have disagreed more with Paul on the role of works in the life of faith, wrote, "True devotion, the kind that is pure and faultless before God the Father, is this: to care for orphans and widows in their difficulties and to keep the world from contaminating us." Orphans and widows were those who were considered worthless by society in that time and place.

Who would that be for us today? Is it someone who is homeless, mentally ill, a drug addict? Is it someone on welfare who just can't seem to find a job? Is it a family whose members don't speak English and whose status is undocumented? Who are the people to whom our world tells us we owe nothing?

Whatever our answer is, that's the person we must welcome, and the warmth of that welcome is what we will be judged by. Plan accordingly.

God, help me look past the labels my culture puts on others and see your beloved children. Help me let go of my opinion about who deserves my help and be welcoming to all. Amen.

25. An Imperfect Hero

2 Samuel 24:21-25

David was one of the greatest heroes in the Bible, but he certainly wasn't perfect. The incident with Bathsheba, described in today's Scripture, showed just how human he was; in fact, that incident represented a turning point in David's life.

Up until that time, David had known nothing but success. He had gone from being the youngest son in a sheep-herding family to being the king of a united Israel, conquering Jerusalem and establishing it as the capital. Then, at the pinnacle of his success, David tried to use his royal power to make an inconvenient situation go away.

After he committed adultery with Bathsheba and murdered her husband, Uriah, everything went downhill. The child conceived through adultery died. Bathsheba later gave birth to Solomon, who succeeded David as king, but that didn't end the couple's grief over their lost child. David's son Amnon raped his half-sister Tamar. Another son, Absalom, started a rebellion against his father. David successfully defended his throne, but Absalom was killed, and David did not rejoice in the victory. There was another rebellion, followed by famine, a war with the Philistines, and a plague. Talk about a run of bad luck!

In the last chapter of 2 Samuel, we find David taking action to atone for his sins and end the plague. Interestingly, this story comes after David uttered his last words. Someone in the editorial department did not do their job.

To atone for his sins and end the plague, David decided to build an altar to the Lord at Jebus, on a place that had been used as a threshing floor by a man named Araunah. Since David couldn't build anything on the land without owning the property, he offered to buy the threshing floor from Araunah.

Araunah could hardly believe that someone as famous and important as David, the man God had anointed as king, was standing there in front of him. What an honor that David would even speak to him! When Araunah learned that David wanted to build an altar so that the plague would end, he was even more impressed. How could he ask the king for money at a time like this? Wasn't it his patriotic duty to give the king what he needed? What's more, it was clearly what God required. The honest, humble Araunah didn't think twice about handing everything over to David, making his sacrifice as a loyal citizen of Israel.

But David's trials had taught him a few things. The arrogant man—the one who had had an affair with a married woman and had thought he could do no wrong—was gone. David had been humbled by his experiences and had experienced more than his share of loss. He knew that he could accept Araunah's offer, and that no one would think any less of David for doing so. Nevertheless, David insisted on paying. He said to Araunah, "I will buy them from you at a fair price. I won't offer up to the LORD my God entirely burned offerings that cost me nothing" (2 Samuel 24:24).

David completed the transaction, built the altar, offered the sacrifices, and ended the plague. The purchase, one of his last official acts as king, demonstrated that although he had greater responsibilities than anyone else, the rules applied to him just as they did to anyone else. The power and authority of his office were not David's to use as he saw fit. He was entrusted with what he had been given, as we are, to use for God's purposes.

It had taken a long time and a lot of heartache, but David finally got it.

Lord, help me give from the depths of my heart. Let me not hold back from you even the things that are most valuable to me. Help me not to take shortcuts but to trust you always. Amen.

26. THE THIRD SERVANT

Matthew 25:14-29; Romans 12:1

I've always felt bad for the third servant in the Parable of the Talents. On a purely practical level, the master didn't leave the servants any instructions. He just gave them the money and left on his journey. Clearly the first two servants were entrepreneurial types, willing to take risks (they'd be great church planters), but the third servant was more cautious. What's more, the master seemed to be shady in his business dealings: he "harvests grain where he hasn't sown." The third servant could have lost all the money, but instead he saved it. Given all these extenuating circumstances, couldn't he just have gotten an "incomplete"?

Parables are stories that intentionally don't contain complete information. They purposely include loose ends, to invite questions and conversation, and it may be that someone who heard Jesus tell the story asked some of the same questions I have. There is no record of such a follow-up conversation, but that's also probably intentional. We're meant to ask questions and discuss it together.

Setting aside some troubling questions about the ethics of the master, who in the story seems to stand in for God, the parable

85

suggests an implicit trust placed in us with every gift we receive from God. We are given those gifts for the purpose of sharing them and blessing others.

It's no coincidence that *talent*, an ancient measure of mass that was used to determine the value of precious metals, is the same word we use today to describe an aptitude or ability. Whether the word represents an amount of money or a certain skill, it's a gift from God that we are intended to use.

When I was doing youth ministry, one girl in our youth group was extremely shy and quiet. She was in an awkward phase of maturing, wasn't considered pretty by society's standards, and didn't quite understand the rules of social interaction, so she usually chose to sit quietly in the group to avoid being ridiculed. But, we discovered, this quiet girl had an amazing singing voice.

We cautiously urged the girl to share her gift, knowing how tough it can be when teenagers are afraid of being embarrassed. Over time, with encouragement, she tentatively agreed to sing in the Youth Sunday worship. She was extremely nervous and later told us that she considered staying home, but as soon as she stood at the microphone in front of the congregation, something clicked. That morning, her angelic voice helped the church experience the presence of the Holy Spirit.

Whether we've been given a good singing voice, the ability to lead, or the underrated gift of a smile and a kind word, these talents are entrusted to us so that we can use them to bless others. Sharing those gifts is only arrogant if we seek glory for ourselves. If our goal is to bless someone and help them grow closer to God, then we're using God's gifts and following our call to use them.

In Romans 12:1, the apostle Paul encourages us "to offer your bodies as living sacrifices to God," out of gratitude for the grace and mercy that God has bestowed upon us. Everything we have should be offered in the service of God.

What gifts has God given you? Is there anything holding you back from being a living sacrifice in the service of God's kingdom?

God, show me how to use the gifts you've given me in your service. Help me overcome any anxiety or shyness and fully trust the ways you have empowered me. Let my sacrifice be acceptable and pleasing in your sight. Amen.

27. Hedging Our Bets

Acts 5:1-11; Malachi 3:8-10

Ananias and Sapphira, described in today's Scripture, could be the basis for either the best or the worst stewardship sermon ever, depending on how the subject is handled. Lifted out of context, it can be preached as "Give to us or God will get you!" But if we read what comes before and after, a different picture emerges.

Ananias and Sapphira were converts in the early church. We don't know if they were present on the day of Pentecost or when they had joined, but clearly something about the new movement had captivated them so much that they decided to sell a piece of land and give the money to the apostles. Yes, they were contributing to the work of God, but they also were hedging their bets by holding some of the proceeds back. After all, if the Christians turned out to be nuts, the two converts would at least have something to show for it. Seen in a purely practical light, their decision made sense.

But the kingdom of God tends to shatter our notions of what is practical, realistic, and fair. It leads us to take steps we otherwise would have thought foolish, and to achieve things we never thought possible. The undoing of Ananias and Sapphira was not their practicality, nor really even their lack of faith. It was their deception—their desire to look good in the eyes of other people and not to take seriously the idea that God knew their hearts.

What would have happened if Ananias and Sapphira had made the same decision to hold back part of the proceeds but had been honest about it? Maybe Ananias would have pulled Peter aside and said, "Look, we think you guys are onto something here, and we're really happy to make a contribution. The thing is, Pete, we also have to think about our future. I'm pretty sure you guys are the real deal, but we've seen messiahs come and go. You're a smart guy, I'm sure you can understand us putting a little bit aside, just in case. Give us more time, let us see a few more miracles, and we'll be all in."

Peter might have replied, "Didn't you hear me telling the story about Jesus saying you can't serve two masters? I admire your honesty, but this is an all-or-nothing proposition. Are you on board with what God is doing, or will you continue bowing to the logic of this corrupt and sinful world?"

There's nothing inherently wrong with saving for a rainy day. For most of the church's history, Christians haven't lived in communes or owned our possessions in common. This particular story in Acts isn't necessarily about how real Christians live, but it does teach us about the kind of trust we are to place in one another.

Are we willing to fully commit ourselves to the work of the Kingdom, or will we settle for the esteem of other people and secretly hold something back? The attitude of Ananias and Sapphira was what Dietrich Bonhoeffer called "cheap grace." That's what happens when we say, "God will forgive me," when we really mean "God won't mind; no big deal."

Whatever your level of commitment, be honest about it. Don't pretend you're all-in if you're not. God's patience with us is endless, and our brothers and sisters in the church will, in their best moments, embody that patience and help bring us along. But we won't help anybody, least of all ourselves, if we're not honest or if we hold back while pretending we're all in.

We can't deceive God. In the end, the only people we're deceiving is ourselves.

Lord, help me be completely honest with myself and others. Give me the courage to admit where I am in my faith journey. Let my honesty pave the way for growth into the disciple you know I can be. Amen.

28. GOD GIVES

John 3:16; Matthew 6:2

Why do we give? Because God gives.

God brought all things into being by giving a simple word. God gave order to the chaos and brought forth life. God took a handful of dirt and gave it life by breathing into it. God gave the first human being a companion, a place to live, and a job to do. When the humans messed up, God continued to give, making clothes for them out of animal skins and continuing his presence, even if it was very different from before.

To the descendants of those first humans, God gave a promise of hope, of land, of a future. God gave a childless octogenarian nomad a name, a family, a place to call home. God gave his descendants a liberator, a guide through the wilderness, and laws teaching them how to live in harmony with God and each other.

God gave judges, prophets, and even the occasional king to guide the people. God gave never-ending patience with the people's rebellious ways. When things started to fall apart, God promised that though there would be dark days, God would one day give in a way that God had never given before.

God gave us himself by becoming one of us. "God so loved the world that he gave his one and only Son." Through the Son, God gave teaching, stories, healing, challenges, and more than a few mysteries we still ponder to this day. The Son gave himself fully to the violence we created in the world. God gave us the Resurrection as proof that the violence and death of our world do not have the last word.

God gave us the church. God gave the church a job to do. God gave the Holy Spirit to empower us in doing that work. God continues to give the church life and new direction, even as we misunderstand, set our own agendas, and generally mess up the good things God has given us.

God gives. And *forgives*. Then God forgives some more. The very fact that we know anything about God is itself a gift from God.

Remember when God gave life to the first humans? We are told that those humans, and by extension all of us, were created in God's image. We were created to be like God. God gives, and so we give. Giving is not an option. It's an inescapable reality of who we are.

We give by sharing our resources, trusting that God will guide the community of faith to do God's redeeming work in the world. We give our time and our energy to this work. We give our presence in the life of the church, to enrich our own lives and the lives of others. We give our prayers, trusting that God works miracles in the world.

Everything that ever has been is now, and will always be, a gift from God. God gives. And so we give.

Lord, help me to be thankful for every gift you give, big and small. Let me never lose my wonder and gratitude for all you have given. Help me to give as freely and generously as you give. Amen.